W9-AGH-810

A Home in the Rain Forest

By Christine Taylor-Butler

Children's Press®
A Division of Scholastic Inc.
New York Toronto London Auckland Sydney
Mexico City New Delhi Hong Kong
Danbury, Connecticut

These content vocabulary word builders are for grades 1–2.
Subject Consultant: Susan Woodward, Professor of Geography, Radford University, Radford, Virginia

Reading Consultant: Cecilia Minden-Cupp, PhD, Former Director of the Language and Literacy
Program, Harvard Graduate School of Education, Cambridge, Massachusetts

Photographs © 2007: Corbis Images: cover background (Royalty-Free), 5 bottom left, 14 (Brian A.
Vikander); Index Stock Imagery/Canstock Images Inc.: back cover, 4 top, 8; Minden Pictures: cover left
inset, 5 top left, 11 (Tui De Roy), 21 top (Gerry Ellis), 5 top right, 7, 20 top, 23 bottom right (Michael
& Patricia Fogden), 5 bottom right, 17 (Frans Lanting), 19 (Claus Meyer), 23 top right (Mark Moffett),
23 top left (Konrad Wothe), 21 bottom (Norbert Wu); Photo Researchers, NY: 23 bottom left (William
Ervin), 20 bottom (Dan Guravich), cover center inset, 4 bottom right, 13 (Jany Sauvanet); photolibrary.
com/Michael Fogden: cover right inset, 2, 15; Visuals Unlimited/Jacques Jangoux: 1, 4 bottom left, 9.

Book Design: Simonsays Design!
Book Production: The Design Lab

Library of Congress Cataloging-in-Publication Data

Taylor-Butler, Christine.
    A home in the rain forest / by Christine Taylor-Butler.
    p. cm. — (Scholastic news nonfiction readers)
    Includes index.
    ISBN-10: 0-516-25347-6
    ISBN-13: 978-0-516-25347-3
    1. Rain forest ecology—Juvenile literature. I. Title. II. Series.
QH541.5.R27T42 2006
577.34—dc22   2006002307

Copyright © 2007 by Scholastic Inc.
All rights reserved. Published simultaneously in Canada.
Printed in the United States of America. 44

CHILDREN'S PRESS and associated logos are trademarks and/or registered trademarks
of Scholastic Library Publishing. SCHOLASTIC and associated logos are trademarks
and/or registered trademarks of Scholastic Inc.

1 2 3 4 5 6 7 8 9 10 R 16 15 14 13 12 11 10 09 08 07

CONTENTS

Central Arkansas Library System
Sue Cowan Williams Branch
Little Rock, Arkansas

WORD HUNT

Look for these words as you read. They will be in **bold**.

habitat
(**hab**-uh-tat)

rain forest
(**rayn for**-ist)

shrubs
(**shruhbz**)

harpy eagles
(**har**-pee **ee**-guhlz)

jaguar
(**ja**-gwar)

sloths
(**sloths**)

tapirs
(**tay**-puhrz)

5

What Is This Place?

There are so many trees that you can hardly see the sky. It's very hot and damp.

A **jaguar** sneaks through the bushes. A snake slithers across a tree branch.

Where are we?

Jaguars are wildcats.

We're in a tropical **rain forest** in South America!

A rain forest is a type of **habitat**. A habitat is where a plant or animal usually lives.

habitat

A tropical rain forest is warm all year long.

From top to bottom, the rain forest is filled with animals.

Harpy eagles build nests at the tops of the tallest trees. They fly high above the treetops. So do bats and hawks.

Harpy eagles use their huge claws to catch snakes, birds, and monkeys.

The next level down is the tops of shorter trees. This level is like a giant roof made of leaves!

Most rain forest animals live in the tops of these trees. **Sloths**, monkeys, and snakes are just a few!

Sloths move very slowly.

Shrubs and the smallest trees are home to red-eyed tree frogs. Lizards and beautiful butterflies also live in these shady areas.

shrubs

A red-eyed tree frog has feet that help it stick to branches and leaves.

Which animals spend their time on the forest floor? Insects do. Large animals such as anteaters and **tapirs** also live there.

Tapirs are related to rhinoceroses.

The rain forest is an exciting place to explore! Check out everything from the tallest trees to the forest floor! You'll meet this anaconda and other amazing animals that live in this habitat!

A DAY IN THE LIFE OF A SLOTH

How does a sloth spend most of its time? A sloth hangs in the trees.

What does a sloth eat? A sloth eats leaves and fruit that grow on trees.

What are a sloth's enemies? Harpy eagles and jaguars are a sloth's enemies.

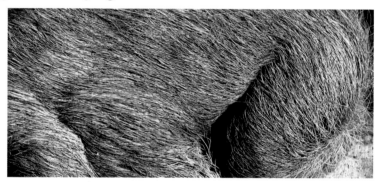

Does a sloth have a special survival trick? A sloth blends in with its surroundings. Green plants called algae grow on a sloth's fur. This makes a sloth blend in with the leaves.

YOUR NEW WORDS

habitat (**hab**-uh-tat) the place where a plant or animal usually lives

harpy eagles (**har**-pee **ee**-guhlz) large, powerful eagles that live in Central America and South America

jaguar (**ja**-gwar) a large spotted cat known for its speed and strength

rain forest (**rayn for**-ist) a tropical forest that receives a great deal of rainfall

shrubs (**shruhbz**) short, woody plants that usually grow close to the ground

sloths (**sloths**) large, slow-moving animals that spend most of their time in the trees

tapirs (**tay**-puhrz) large, pig-shaped animals that have short trunks

OTHER ANIMALS THAT LIVE IN THE RAIN FOREST

iguanas

leaf-cutter ants

tarantulas

toucans

23

INDEX

FIND OUT MORE

Book:
Greenwood, Elinor. *Rain Forest.* New York: DK Publishing, 2001.

Website:
Rain Forest Heroes
http://www.rainforestheroes.com/

MEET THE AUTHOR:

Christine Taylor-Butler is the author of twenty-four fiction and nonfiction books for children. A graduate of the Massachusetts Institute of Technology, Christine now lives in Kansas City, Missouri, with her husband, two daughters, a pride of mischievous black cats, and two tanks of fish.